Dear Family of Earth,

2020 taught us we can't always control life, but each of us can:
1. do our part
2. look after loved ones
3. smile through hard times together

Ready to discover more contagious but great things each of us can choose to control the spread of?

Read on and BE ONE!
Kelly Thornhill

THE WORLD STAYED HOME TOGETHER
First edition, published 2020

By Kelly Thornhill

Copyright © 2020, Kelly Thornhill

Softcover ISBN-13: 978-1-952685-00-2
Hardcover ISBN-13: 978-1-942661-57-3

All rights reserved. No part of this book may be reproduced or transmitted in any form or by any means, electronic or mechanical, including photocopying, recording or by any information storage and retrieval system, without written permission from the author, except for the inclusion of brief quotations in a review.

Published by Kitsap Publishing
Poulsbo, WA 98370
www.KitsapPublishing.com

HUMANITY

Our DNA scientifically proves
we all belong to one another,
as one big Family of Earth,
but it is our HUMANITY
that brings us together.

HUMANITY

Our DNA scientifically proves
we all belong to one another,
as one big Family of Earth,
but it is our HUMANITY
that brings us together.

The year started off
just like any other.

When suddenly
life quickly changed.

Schools, churches, and stores began
closing, and sports seasons ended.

It was like everything was on pause.

All around the world

we were told to

do what was best for

everyone

everywhere

and stay

safe

at home.

Each of us sacrificed

our daily freedoms

and many gave up money

to protect

each other

from getting sick.

While most people stayed home,
some had jobs that helped us
remain comfortable, fed,
and learning.

Others tirelessly cared for
all who got sick.

We grew more grateful
for each person that served us.

The hearts and minds
of people all over the world
came together
in LOVE,
creating the biggest
act of global UNITY
the world has ever known.

Our HUMANITY remembered
we belong to one another,
and
we all need each other.

We learned
every single one of us
needs to do their part
to make a difference
TOGETHER.

- Part One -
Humanity, Unity & Our Beauty Within

What does HUMANITY mean?

DEFINITION

HUMANITY – the *bond* of sharing that *connects all* humans; belonging together; our collective identity; the core of human values with their quality being humane goodness.

HUMANITY

In South Africa, the word for HUMANITY is Ubuntu.

It means all of HUMANITY is invisibly bound together in ways that make us ONE.

The only way to have success is sharing ourselves with others and caring for one another like they are a part of ourselves.

WE are all in this together.

HUMANITY

HUMANITY's bond of sharing
includes every single one of us.

HUMANITY

Synonyms:

Promise
Pledge
Oath
Word
Tie
Link
Connection
Union

HUMANITY

HUMANITY is the WE in all of us
and the WE inside each of us.
WE see ourselves in each other.
It is an inner sense of goodness
that brings out the best in us.
WE see the needs of others
and do our part to help.
Our 'WE over ME' choices make
us beautiful,
our bond stronger,
and the world a better place.

HUMANITY

When this bond between us is strong,
we thrive in UNITY.
Our HUMANITY draws us together
by helping us feel included,
cared for, happy,
healthy, and safe.

Our UNITY increases harmony, charity, ability, longevity, prosperity, and liberty.

What does UNITY mean?

DEFINITION

UNITY – thriving together, a civilized state of being joined to one whole with mutual caring, peace, justice, and progress; oneness of heart, mind and purpose.

UNITY

"Though we cannot think alike,
may we not love alike?
May we not be of one heart,
though we are not of one opinion?

Without all doubt,
we may."

John Wesley
1703 - 1791

UNITY

To BE ONE

does not mean

everyone should be the same

or have the same opinions

(how boring would that be).

To BE ONE mind

is to see one another as HUMAN,

with valuable differences but

mostly the same as ourselves.

UNITY

Like musicians in an orchestra,
or different players on one team,
global pandemics are
only resolved altogether.
To BE ONE remembers we are all
one family with the common goal
of being better together.
When we value ONENESS over
individual success, we get both.

UNITY

We Need One Another

UNITY

To BE ONE heart,

sometimes said, "ONE LOVE",

refers to universal love and respect

from all people

for all people.

No one is excluded.

To be UNIFIED with ONE heart means

treating everyone like they belong.

UNITY

BE ONE

What does INNER BEAUTY mean?

DEFINITION

INNER BEAUTY – *builds lasting bonds* between people; made of attributes of peace and love; within all people to grow; attractive and admired character traits; cannot fade with age; choices that bring happiness to others, benevolence, altruism, amiability; reduces suffering and violence.

INNER BEAUTY

Our shared bond of HUMANITY
flows between all of us,
and starts inside each of us.

INNER BEAUTY

2020 reminded mankind to first take time to STOP.

INNER BEAUTY

We were born with everything we need

inside us

to take mankind to a better place.

Our goodness comes out

by doing what we came here for.

INNER BEAUTY

We grow our beauty within
by letting it out.

What does L♥VE mean?

DEFINITION

LOVE – power or energy of unselfish attention that attracts and connects us together.

LOVE

LOVE is

the heart of being HUMAN.

L O V E

LOVE starts within.

Our unkind thoughts make us droop,
but LOVE nurtures us with kindness.

L O V E

Whatever we focus our attention on,

our LOVE for that magnifies.

That is why

we grow to LOVE the people we serve.

L O V E

LOVE is a powerful magnetic-like energy

within us

that attracts caring attention

between us.

LOVE

LOVE leads us to joy by turning us inside-out,
thinking about ourselves less,
and others more.

L O V E

LOVE remembers we belong to each other, and is the glue that holds us together.

What does PEACE mean?

DEFINITION

PEACE – (Greek 'eirene' from verb 'eiro') to *join* or *bind together* that which has been separated; harmony from *joining* into a *whole*, relieving suffering from the broken, or divided.

P E A C E

'Pieces' are not what PEACE is,
but 'to piece together' is.

PEACE

PEACE starts with UNITY within.

If what we think, say, and do
do not all agree,
we feel weak and broken inside.

PEACE

PEACE knows what is needed to make us whole again.

P E A C E

Peace actively works to make
coming together possible,
even when it is not easy.

P E A C E

PEACE is understanding, fairness, and friendship.

The more LOVE we add, the more PEACE we have.

PEACE

PEACE remembers everyone belongs,

and does what it takes to
help us BE ONE again.

- Part Two -
Meet Peace & Love and Their Children

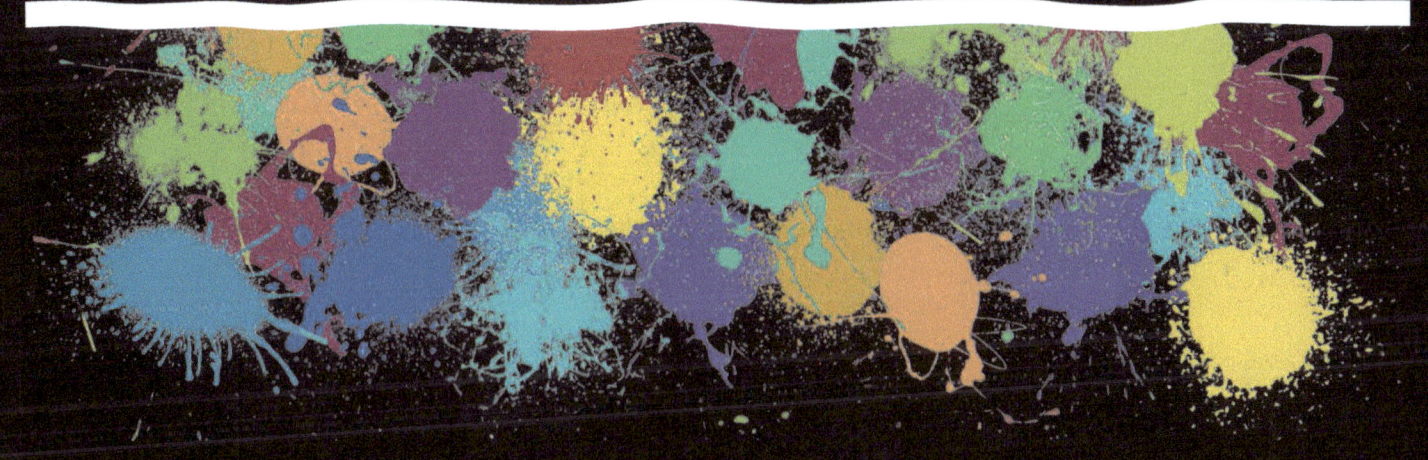

To better understand
the BEAUTY of our HUMANITY,
imagine
PEACE and LOVE
as parents
whose children
together make up
their characteristics.

Peace

I am Peace.

I like bridges instead of walls

because bridges bring people together

just as building friendships

makes sadness go away.

I help us all get along.

I also take time to quietly connect

with the good around and within me,

enjoying beauty and life's little things.

I say sorry and forgive,

cleaning out my inner clutter.

Doing this pops my trouble bubble,

clearing my flow, settling my soul,

helping me feel whole.

I am Love.

I see everyone as a part of one big family.

I believe that each person is uniquely valuable, and all are equal, good, and worthy of my attention.

My energy has no boundaries.

My reasons are unselfish.

My concern is how others are.

I notice how my heart feels inside, making sure is stays soft, open, warm and fills up the front of my chest, not small, hard and shrinking back.

My daily connections with people give me meaning, purpose, and a very happy life.

1
Compassion

I am Compassion.

I care about how other people feel.

I try to imagine myself in their shoes to understand what they are going through.

I never: Compare, Criticize, Categorize, or Compete,

because underneath it all,

we all belong to each other.

I am Courage.

and I can do hard things.

People may laugh, but I still do them.

Even though I am not perfect,

I am not ashamed to keep trying.

I do my best to be a champion for good,

like being a friend to someone not like me.

3
Curiosity

I am Curiosity.

I like to open doors
and walk down hallways,
always curious about what is ahead
or around the corner.

To me, the world is full of interesting people
with amazing stories.

Every new day brings new wonders.

4

Dignity

I am Dignity.

I am worthy of love and belonging,

and so is everyone.

I treat myself and others with respect.

I listen carefully when others talk,

and honor them with good manners.

I care about freedom

and for the beauty all around me.

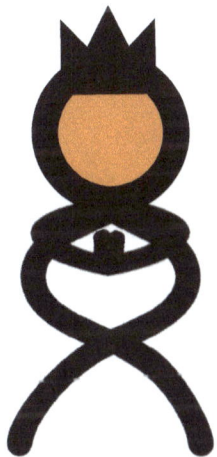

5
Gratitude

I am Gratitude.

I am thankful for big things and little things.

I am thankful for the food I eat,

the people who care for me,

and for our beautiful earth.

I am thankful for friends and teachers

and for everything I can learn.

I show my thanks by trying my best.

6
Humility

I am Humility.

I do not show off or brag.

I do not have to be right, first, or the best
to feel good about myself.

I can be very happy for other people,
can admit my mistakes and forgive others.

I know I can always learn more,
and by doing these things, I grow joyfully.

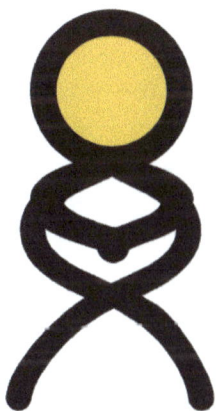

7
Integrity

I am Integrity.

I think a lot about right and wrong.

My inner self grows bigger and stronger with every good choice I make.

If I think something is right,

or I say I will do something, I do it.

I know what I do affects others.

People can trust me to choose the right.

8
Involvement

I am Involvement.

I like to help, to do my part,

and to be a part of things.

It is true that many hands make light work.

Participation makes me happy.

Working with people helps me make

all sorts of different types of friends

and learn different types of things.

I am Kindness.

In words and actions and thoughts,

my goal is always to help

and never harm anything or anyone.

People say I have a contagious super-power.

Being nice makes everyone

magically feel better

which makes them want to be nice too.

10
Mercy

I am Mercy.

Sometimes people hurt me by mistake, and sometimes they do on purpose. Either way, I do not let my heart shrink toward them and be angry. I know we are all learning. Love and forgiving helps us grow better than anything in the world.

11
Optimism

I am Optimism.

I love life and all it promises.

I see the best in myself and others,

and I believe that anything is possible.

People want to be around me

because my hopeful confidence helps them

discover the beauty of life too.

12
Responsibility

I am Responsibility.
I am steady and dependable.
If you give me a job to do,
you can count on me to do it.
I do not blame, or complain,
and I do not procrastinate
because I care about who I am helping,
and care about becoming my best self.

13
Sincerity

I am Sincerity.

I am true to who I am
and honest in everything I say or do.
People like that about me and trust me.
I think about the difference between
real and fake.
I like real because even though it is less
perfect, it is more useful and valuable.

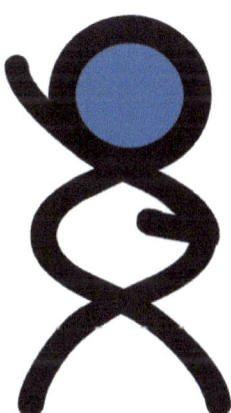

14

Tolerance

I am Tolerance.

Many of my friends come from different backgrounds and different places, with different-sounding names and different-looking faces.

I have learned how much we are alike.

I do not judge because I am a safe place.

People are free to be themselves around me.

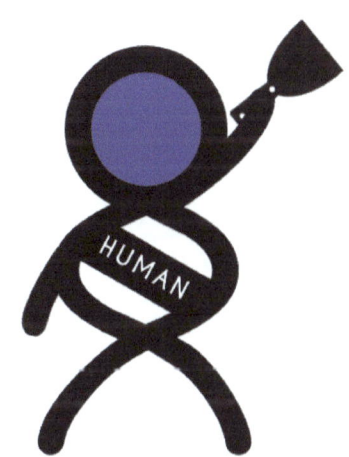

15
Wisdom

I am Wisdom.

I think about life and learn about choice and consequence.

I am learning to control my thoughts, my feelings, and what to feed my body.

I choose good friends and treat others the way they would want to be treated.

My choices lead to happiness.

COMPASSION

COURAGE

CURIOSITY

DIGNITY

GRATITUDE

HUMILITY

INTEGRITY

INVOLVEMENT

 KINDNESS

 MERCY

 OPTIMISM

 RESPONSIBILITY

 SINCERITY

 TOLERANCE

 WISDOM

Developing my INNER BEAUTY of PEACE and LOVE transforms me into my best and happiest self.

COMPASSION
COURAGE
CURIOSITY
DIGNITY
GRATITUDE
HUMILITY
INTEGRITY
INVOLVEMENT
KINDNESS
MERCY
OPTIMISM
RESPONSIBILITY
SINCERITY
TOLERANCE
WISDOM

Reaching out to connect with others helps them see who they really are by letting them see who I really am.

I am enough.
I am made of goodness.

I believe that I am,
and will behave like I am.

Each of us is HOPE for a better future together.

May you tap into your inner beauty and make your life a message of what humanity means everywhere you go.

Kelly Thornhill is the founder of Family of Earth, a company celebrating our origins and connection to one another. Kelly grew up in a household that embraced the importance of personal growth and strong moral character. Her larger-than-life father was an energetic warrior-philosopher from Liverpool, England with boundless compassion and unquenchable curiosity. He was a student of the human condition, whose position with the Canadian Air Force took his family to every part of Canada. The many moves helped Kelly overcome a natural shyness, to reach beyond her comfort zone and overcome her fears. Kelly learned to search beyond apparent differences to discover the unique qualities of human goodness that both set us apart and connect us.

As an adult, Kelly is a writer, designer, entrepreneur, homemaker, and has been serving over 30 years in youth leadership roles, as a teacher, mentor, and counselor. Kelly is a deep thinker with a pure heart whose life mission is a message of love and peace, and whose greatest joy and growth has been as a wife and mother of five. Kelly lives with her husband and youngest son in Flower Mound, Texas, USA.

Visit her at familyofearth.com.

www.ingramcontent.com/pod-product-compliance
Lightning Source LLC
Chambersburg PA
CBHW051348110526
44591CB00025B/2941